LAKERS

JERRY WEST

by Paul J. Deegan

Illustrated by Harold Henriksen

Text copyright © 1974 by Amēcus Street. Illustration copyright © 1974 by Creative Education.
International copyrights reserved in all countries. No part of this book may be reproduced in any
form without written permission from the publisher. Printed in the United States.

Library of Congress Number: 73-19525   ISBN: 0-87181-311-9

Published by Creative Education, Mankato, Minnesota 56001
Prepared for the Publisher by Amēcus Street
Distributed by Childrens Press, 1224 West Van Buren Street, Chicago, Illinois 60607

Library of Congress Cataloging in Publication Data

Deegan, Paul J   1937
    Jerry West.
    (Creative's superstars)
    SUMMARY: A brief biography of the star of the Los Angeles Lakers basketball team who holds
many scoring records.
    1. West, Jerry, 1938-   — Juvenile literature. (1. West, Jerry, 1938-   2. Basketball —
Biography) I. Henriksen, Harold, illus. II. Title.
GV884-W4D43   796.32'3'0924 (B) (92)   73-19525
ISBN 0-87191-311-9

The 12-year-old boy wanted to play on his junior high school football team. Jerry West was about 5-feet, 6-inches tall but he weighed less than 100 pounds. The coach at the school in tiny Cheylan, West Virginia, wouldn't give him a uniform. He was too small.

Several weeks later Jerry West went out for the junior high basketball team. This time he stayed on the team. But he dressed for only a few games and played in none.

The boy who couldn't make it as a 7th grader at a school in a town of only 500 people became one of the 2 or 3 best backcourt men ever to play basketball. He is right up there with Bob Cousy and Oscar Robertson.

How did Jerry West become a superstar?

First of all, like many boys, he grew a lot. When he became taller and stronger, he also began to display unusual athletic talent. Among other things, he is very quick. He also has unusually long arms. The extra reach was to be valuable for he would not grow exceptionally tall—6-feet, 2-inches by his last year in high school, an inch more later.

West is known as a scorer and by the time he was 16 he was already a great shooter. He had a good eye and a soft touch. He had first started throwing up baskets in a neighbor's backyard when he was so young that he had to use both hands and toss the ball

underhanded. He kept going back to that outdoor dirt court. He shot for hours. Sometimes he was punished when he forgot to come home for supper. Rain, cold, snow—he kept on shooting.

This willingness to work probably tells more about why Jerry West became a great basketball player than the fact that he grew to average size for an athlete. There have been many pro guards who were taller and stronger than West. But few, probably none, work harder.

West has been described as nervous, intense, a perfectionist. He thinks a lot about his play and expects a lot of himself. He knows that after playing basketball for 23 years, he can't be sharp for every game. He has played over 1,000 basketball games in high school, at the University of West Virginia, and for the Los Angeles Lakers. The Lakers play over 100 games a year. Pre-season games begin in September and the playoff finals run into May.

Even though West knows that he will sometimes have an off night, such performances irritate him. He always wants to play well. He also believes in going all-out when he's playing. It's silly to talk about "giving

110 percent," West has said. But he aims for 100 per cent effort. He has said that being able to give a good 2nd or even 3rd effort during a game marks the difference between the good player and the ordinary one.

Many years ago, Bill Russell called West a "digger." Now coach and general manager of the Seattle SuperSonics, Russell said West is "fierce." He cited West's hustle and clutch play, saying West "seldom misses down the stretch." Russell said West worked hard at basketball "because he wants to be great."

West's attitude, effort, and considerable talent have brought him from a little town in west-central West Virginia to Los Angeles — an area where nearly 7 million people live. His reported $300,000 a year salary far removes him from the high school boy in Cheylan who didn't give much thought to college because he knew his parents couldn't afford the cost. Today Jerry, his wife, Jane, and their three boys live in a large, new house in the stylish Brentwood section of Los Angeles. He has the things desired by a great many people—success, admiration, recognition, money.

However, he has paid a price for these things. Often he has walked onto the basketball court sick or injured. Although he is 6-feet, 3-inches, and weighs 185 to 190 pounds, West is a relatively small man in pro basketball. It is a game where men several inches taller and 50 pounds heavier are agile and active players.

West's nose has been broken 10 times—the first 2 times in college. A torn knee resulted in surgery in 1971. Twice West has broken his hand. His fingers have been broken and sprained. He has had teeth knocked out, an eyeball bruised. His joints and muscles have been twisted, sprained, and pulled countless times.

The travel—thousands of miles a year—as well as the games are wearing. So is the tension involved in playing. West doesn't like to take pills. But he finds himself taking pills to keep from being sick before a game or to sleep following a game.

Has his success and the demands of pro basketball changed Jerry West? Many who know him say no. He remains one of the most popular professional athletes in the country. His public image is still that of the friendly, small-town sports hero. Fans seem to identify with Jerry's determined manner on the court and his quiet life away from basketball.

Jerry's wife and friends say that off the court his nervousness shows up. He doesn't like to sit still and is uncomfortable spending much time in the same place. The three West boys—David, now 2; Michael, 10; and Mark, 9—can keep him busy when he's home. Jerry is associated with a summer basketball camp. He also spends many hours on the golf course. He learned to hunt and fish as a boy in West Virginia and still turns to these activities for relaxation. One of his favorite fishing partners runs a food counter in a drug store near the campus of UCLA in the Westwood area of Los Angeles. Hollis Johnson's Fountain and Grill is a sports hangout and West often drops by to talk sports. Jerry is a sports fan himself. He attends many of the pro basketball, football, and hockey games in Los Angeles.

The things West likes to do are the same things enjoyed by millions of other people. This is one reason why so many different people can identify with West . . . the movie stars who come to Lakers' games; Hollis Johnson, several years older than Jerry; and the short-haired factory worker who watches the Lakers only on TV.

West, of course, is not the same shy boy who went from Cheylan to the University of West Virginia in the fall of 1956. The West Virginia twang still comes out when he's excited. But the crew-cut has long since given way to a modest brush-cut. Though still quiet in public, West no longer lacks confidence in his basketball skills. He knows that he is a great ballplayer and that many people admire him. Yet, it is said, he still finds it hard to believe that this success all came his way.

The success includes an ability to get along with so many different types of people, fellow athletes includ-

ed. Not all superstars are well liked by other players. West is also one of the few white superstars in basketball. Sixty per cent of the pro players and most of the best ones are black. Yet West has been popular with his teammates and opponents, blacks and whites, throughout his long pro career.

This popularity with other players was evident early in his life. He was elected captain of the Cheylan junior high team when he was a 9th grader. The success, though, came slower. And there were letdowns along the way. Jerry had gotten into some games as an 8th grader after not playing at all in 7th grade. A starter as a 9th grader, he averaged 13 points a game.

From Cheylan he went to East Bank high school. Cheylan was very small. Only 500 people lived there. East Bank, 4 miles away, was a large regional school. The East Bank Pioneers played in what many people thought was the toughest basketball league in West Virginia.

During the summer before he entered East Bank as a 10th grader, Jerry grew . . . and grew . . . and grew. The small 9th grader was a tall 10th grader. He had grown 6 inches to 6 feet. Unfortunately, the sudden growth left him clumsy and awkward. He did make the high school team but didn't play much. The season ended early when he suffered his first basketball injury, a broken ankle.

As an 11th grader, Jerry had shed much of the clumsiness of the previous year. He made the starting 5 at East Bank and became the team's leading scorer. Jerry has said that he probably shot as well then as he ever has. He had a good eye and a soft touch. Anyone who has watched West play as a pro can picture him with the ball. He stops suddenly and almost in the same instant goes straight into the air for his best shot—a jumper from 10 to 15 feet. Professional players talk about West's "quick release"—the speed with which he gets his shot off. He didn't have that mastered in high school, but he could score. He averaged over 24 points a game as an 11th grader for a team that won only 11 of 24 games. He scored 38 points in one game, 37 in another.

After that season, Jerry was considered a star athlete. He was still shy and didn't talk much about himself. He wasn't sure what he wanted to do after high school. He did know that somehow he wanted his life to be a success.

The future began to take some direction when colleges began contacting him about playing basketball for them. One coach who came to see Jerry was Fred Schaus, who had started a winning trend at West Virginia University.

Many more coaches were interested in Jerry after his final year at East Bank. Jerry's team lost only 4 games during the regular season and he averaged almost 34 points a game. He scored 35 points or more 8 times, hitting 45 in one game, 40 in another. The East Bank Pioneers continued to do well in the West Virginia state tournament playdowns. They were one of the 4 teams to go into the final round at the university fieldhouse in Morgantown.

The 17-year-old West led his team into the finals by scoring 43 points and grabbing a record 23 rebounds. In the title game against hometown Morgantown high, Jerry continued his exceptional play. He scored 39 points and East Bank won the West Virginia state championship, 71-56.

West had not only led his team to a championship, he was the first West Virginia high school player to score more than 900 points in one season. Now over 60 colleges sought him.

Jerry chose his homestate university. Freshmen could not play varsity basketball at major colleges then. But when the 1957-1958 season began, Jerry, a sophomore, was in the starting lineup. With West playing forward, West Virginia enjoyed 3 fine seasons. The 1957-1958 team may have been the best. The Mountaineers had a big center and lost only one game during the regular season. They were undefeated in their league, the Southern Conference.

Rated the nation's number one college team, West Virginia was favored to win the National Collegiate Athletic Association (NCAA) tournament. They were dumped in the first game of the Eastern Regionals by New York's Manhattan College.

This was the first of many times that good teams on which Jerry played would be sidelined short of a championship. It began to appear in later years that East Bank would be the only championship team on which Jerry would play.

The loss to Manhattan in the spring of 1958 set one pattern for West's career and contradicted another. West has often been called "Mr. Clutch" for

his ability to produce in pressure situations. Time and time again, the Lakers would rely upon him in crucial games. Usually he came through. The pattern had started at East Bank with his great play in the state tournament. But the 1958 tournament loss to Manhattan was not one of Jerry's clutch performances. He picked up 4 fouls in the first half and scored only 10 points in the game.

Jerry had averaged just under 18 points a game for his first college season. He followed this with 2 great seasons in his junior and senior years. An All-American selection both years, West averaged nearly 27 points a game as a junior and over 29 points in his senior year. He broke all the West Virginia scoring records. The Mountaineers won 2 more conference championships and won 22 of 26 regular season games in 1958-1959 and 21 of 25 in 1959-1960.

In Jerry's junior year, West Virginia had moved through the NCAA playoffs into the finals in Louisville, Kentucky. West had scored 28 points against California in the championship game, but West Virginia lost 71-70. Jerry was chosen Most Valuable Player in the tournament.

West and Oscar Robertson, whose Cincinnati team was one of the semi-finalists in the 1959 NCAA tourney, were the first 2 players chosen in the draft of college players by the National Basketball Association

(NBA) in the spring of 1960. West and the "Big O" had been considered the best college players in the country. They had been teammates on the U.S. squad which won the basketball championship in the 1959 Pan-American Games played in Chicago. They were together again on the 1960 United States Olympic basketball team. This was probably the best Olympic basketball team ever. Eight of the 12 U.S. players later played pro basketball. The U.S. team easily won the 8 games they played in the Rome Olympics. They averaged over 100 points a game, defeating Brazil 90-63 for the gold medal.

After the Olympics, West reported to the Lakers and Robertson returned to Cincinnati, where the NBA Royals had picked him. When West was drafted, the Lakers were in Minneapolis. Over the summer, the team's owner had moved the team to Los Angeles and hired a new coach—Fred Schaus, Jerry's college coach.

Not only would Jerry now be playing as a professional, he was also a husband. Before the Olympics, he had married a very pretty girl from Weston, West Virginia—Martha Jane Kane. They met in a class at West Virginia.

The 1960-1961 season was a long one for West. He had no trouble making the Lakers. However, he thought—and still thinks—that he should have been a starter right away. Schaus didn't agree. He thought it was better for Jerry to break in gradually. Jerry played in every Laker game that year. But he didn't start until after mid-season.

The move from college to pro ball was not easy, even for an All-American. One problem was that he was moved from forward, where he had always played, to guard. Though he now weighed around 180 pounds, he was not big enough at 6-feet, 3-inches to play inside in pro ball. He was an excellent shooter and a fine passer. However, defense in the NBA is rougher, players check offensive players with their hands, and most pros

are faster, bigger, and stronger than the average college player. It was harder to get free to shoot and West had to work on his dribbling, which was only fair, and his moves. West did not learn to use his left hand until he became a pro. Even today, after 13 years in the NBA, he seldom goes to his left when he wants to shoot. This weakness would be a serious handicap for most players but West gets by with it. This is because, like most great athletes, he has exceptional foot speed. He starts very fast when he moves with the ball. He drives to the basket so well it doesn't pay to overplay him to stop his outside shot. Through hard work, West has also become an effective, if not stylish, dribbler.

Playing defense was also much tougher in the NBA. It's interesting that West, one of the best scorers ever to play the game, prides himself on his defense. He has said he thinks he's a better defensive than offensive player. Others in the NBA, however, believe that West hasn't spent too much of his playing time worrying about defense. Jerry would disagree. It is true that as the Lakers' scoring leader, West is not often called upon to guard an opponent's best guard. When he is, he works hard.

Pro stars can't be stopped from scoring but West works to keep them from where they want to be. He has studied his opponents and knows what they want to do. West tries to make them do something else. He often appears to be out of position on defense. This, he says, is because he tries to lull a player into feeling he can make a move, a move West has anticipated. Then Jerry closes. Making use of his exceptionally long arms and quickness, he is often able to steal the ball. West also blocks many more shots than would be expected of a player his size. Other pros recognize West's ability to play defense—"He can be very good when he works at it," says one. Several times the NBA players have elected West to the league's All-Defensive team.

Offensive play, though, is where West has made his mark. When the Lakers need points, they go to West. During Jerry's first year in the NBA, the Lakers lost more than half of their regular season games. Still they made the playoffs, as they've done each year West has been a pro.

During his first playoffs in 1961, the 23-year-old West set a pattern that was to mark his pro career. He averaged more points a game than he did during the regular season. He had nearly 23 points a game in the playoffs, 5 points higher than his season's average.

West has said he gets fired up for the playoffs. He admits he tries harder when each game is so important. The result has been that he has scored more playoff points, over 4,000, than any other NBA player. He has also converted more free throws and averaged more points per game in playoffs. Seven times his playoff average has been better than 30 points a game.

Despite this, the Lakers' record during the past 13 seasons—with a single exception—has been marred by their failure to win the league championship. Nine times in those years the Lakers have been in the playoff finals. During the first 10 of those years, they were finalists 7 times. Each time they lost—6 times to Boston, once to New York.

Though the Lakers never went all the way in the 1960's, West had some outstanding playoff games.

A play that West calls "my trophy" came in the 3rd game of the championship series against Boston in 1962. West had hit two jumpers to tie the game.

After the teams formed to put the ball in play, West was guarding Bob Cousy, the Celtics' great star. As the in-bounds pass came to Cousy, West jumped in front of him and grabbed the ball. He raced toward the basket and laid the ball up. As it fell through the net, the buzzer ended the game. The Lakers had won by 2.

In 1965 West became the only player ever to average more than 40 points a game through the entire playoffs. In a 6-game series against Baltimore, which the Lakers won, Jerry scored 49, 52, 44, 48, 43, and 42 points. The 52 points set a one game playoff record for guards.

West set a playoff scoring record of 556 points in 1969 when he was also named the Most Valuable Player in the playoff finals. His 53 points in the first game of the title series against Boston bettered his previous total of 52. During the 5th game of the Boston series, West pulled a hamstring muscle in his left leg. The Lakers lost the 6th game to bring the series into a 7th and deciding game. This game would be at The Forum, the plush arena in suburban Inglewood which has been the Lakers' home court since 1968.

West had to be helped down the stairs to the dressing room before the 7th game. The money player would earn his pay that night. The Lakers trailed by 21 in the 2nd half. West, playing on a leg on which he couldn't even stand a couple of hours before, still wouldn't quit. Amazingly he began hitting from all over the court. Then the Lakers' 7-foot-plus center, Wilt Chamberlain, went out of the game with an injury. Still the Lakers moved closer. They drew within a single point. But they couldn't take the lead. Boston won 108-106. West's 42 points had not been enough.

The Boston players came to Jerry after the game. They tried to say how much they admired his effort. The words were tough to find. Bill Russell, the Celtics player-coach, just grabbed Jerry's hands. John Havlicek told West: "Jerry, I love you."

A year later, 1970, West topped his playoff total points mark by 6 points. He did this even though his hands were so bruised during the championship series that he was sometimes given pain-killing shots. The 3rd game of the finals against New York is another game that Jerry will always remember.

The Lakers and the Knicks had each won a game. Playing in the Forum, Los Angeles trailed by 2 with only a few seconds to play. West had the ball in the back court. Glancing up at the overhead scoreboard, he saw that time was about to run out. He was not yet at the centerline of the court, but he had to shoot. None of the 17,500 fans in The Forum expected the ball to come close to the orange hoop. As the ball started to fall from its high arc, it was surprisingly on target. ("I really thought it would go in after I shot," West said later). Closer, closer it came to the basket. Plunk! It dropped through the rim. Swish! It rolled through the cord. West had made a 63-foot shot. The game was tied. Unfortunately, the Lakers lost in overtime.

West missed the 1971 playoffs, won by the Milwaukee Bucks, because he had surgery after injuring his knee on March 2.

When the 1971-1972 season began, West was playing for his 4th coach in 12 years with the Lakers. Schaus had left coaching in 1967 to become the Lakers' general manager. Bill Van Breda Kolff and Joe Mullaney

had followed him. Now the Lakers' coach was Bill Sharman, the former Boston Celtics' star. Sharman ran hard workouts and held shooting practices on game days. Not all the players liked the work he put them through. But Sharman got things together for the Lakers.

Los Angeles had a super season. They won 33 games in a row in the first months of the season. This was an NBA record. It was also a record for most wins in a row by a pro team in any sport. The Lakers won

the Pacific Division of the NBA's Western Conference by 18 games. They won 69 of their 82 games, also a record. They wiped out their first 1972 playoff opponent, the Chicago Bulls, in 4 straight games. Milwaukee, the defending NBA champion, was next. The Bucks fell in 6 games. Jerry West was in the NBA playoff finals for the 8th time. For the 2nd time in 3 years, the Lakers' opponent was New York.

History did not repeat itself. The Lakers had an easy series. The Knickerbockers won only one game. Los Angeles was finally the NBA champion. This, West has said, was his greatest thrill.

West had been 17 when he played on a high school championship team. Now 17 years later he had played on his 2nd championship team—the world champions of basketball.

There was talk that West might retire after the 1972 season. He had not shot well during the 1972 playoffs. He made only 38 percent of his field goal tries, 10 percent below his career average. For the first time, his playoff scoring average, 23 points a game, was below his regular season's average. Fans were writing and calling him, offering him advice on breaking his slump. Jerry finally determined himself that he was shooting too quickly and wasn't coming straight down on his jumper. On this, his favorite shot, he tries to land on the identical spot from where he takes off.

West might have been tempted to quit as a champion. He was 34 a few weeks after the title game. Fred Schaus was leaving the Lakers' organization to return to college coaching at Purdue University. But when the 1972-1973 season started, Jerry was in the Lakers' lineup. His huge salary was certainly one reason he continued to play. Moreover, basketball is a very important part of his life. Though the season is long and the travel can be tiring, West very much enjoys the life of the pro athlete.

The Lakers' superstar has said that pro athletes are members of a "private club" and no outsider can appreciate what they share together. Those in pro sports, West says, "have two families"—the one at home and the team. The association with teammates in practice and traveling, the constant banter between them, the free time on the road, the buildup of tension on game days, the release of that tension in the movement, contact, and reaction of the game . . . these are things few successful athletes want to put behind them.

During the 1972-1973 season, only 4 players among the more than 300 men playing in the NBA and the American Basketball Association, the rival pro league begun in 1969-1970, were older than Jerry West. The only regular older than West was his teammate, Wilt Chamberlain—36 years old and in his 14th year in the NBA.

West "is supposed to be old," says Spencer Haywood, the Seattle SuperSonics young star, but "he may be the greatest . . . he's so quick it's unbelievable." Herm Gilliam, the Atlanta Hawks' veteran guard, says "I don't see West slowing down one bit." Lakers' Coach Sharman has said that he once took West's play for granted. "Now I feel that he is the most complete player in the game today — maybe of all time."

The 1972-1973 Lakers had a good season. But they won only the first game of the championship playoff series against New York. The Knicks won 4 in a row to take the NBA title away from Los Angeles. Once more the Lakers would spend their summer looking ahead instead of relaxing with a championship.

When the Lakers began the 1973-1974 NBA season, Jerry West was back for a 14th year. He had a full career behind him but would be going all out in hopes of another championship. West had reported late to a team that seemed to be more dependent upon him than ever. Chamberlain had jumped to the rival league and high–scoring forward Jim McMillian had been traded. The Lakers needed West's scoring punch if they were to have a successful season.

At age 35 West was the leading all-time scoring leader among pro guards. His 63 points against New York in 1962 is the most points ever scored by an NBA guard in a game. Three times he has averaged

31 points a game during a season, leading the league in scoring average in 1969-1970. He holds the record for most free throws in one season. He once made 31 in a row. Most of the Lakers' career scoring records are owned by West. He has scored more than 24,000 points as a professional. He satisfied one of the few goals he set for himself as a pro when he passed the 20,000 mark in 1971. Only a handful of NBA players have scored this many points. West is not just a gunner either. He led the NBA in assists per game, an average of over 9 a contest, in 1971-1972.

West has said he is "never satisfied with his play." There is always something he could have improved upon. After 13 years, 9 playoff finals, and one NBA championship, Jerry West is still working to improve.

LAKERS
LAKERS
44
4

JACK NICKLAUS
BILL RUSSELL
MARK SPITZ
VINCE LOMBARDI
BILLIE JEAN KING
ROBERTO CLEMENTE
JOE NAMATH
BOBBY HULL
HANK AARON
JERRY WEST
TOM SEAVER
JACKIE ROBINSON
MUHAMMAD ALI
O. J. SIMPSON
JOHNNY BENCH
WILT CHAMBERLAIN
ARNOLD PALMER
A. J. FOYT
JOHNNY UNITAS
GORDIE HOWE

superstars! superstars! superstars! superstars!

CREATIVE EDUCATION SPORTS SUPERSTARS

WALT FRAZIER
PHIL AND TONY ESPOSITO
BOB GRIESE
FRANK ROBINSON
PANCHO GONZALES
LEE TREVINO
KAREEM ABDUL JABBAR
JEAN CLAUDE KILLY
EVONNE GOOLAGONG
ARTHUR ASHE
SECRETARIAT
ROGER STAUBACK
FRAN TARKENTON
BOBBY ORR
LARRY CSONKA
BILL WALTON
ALAN PAGE
PEGGY FLEMING
OLGA KORBUT
DON SCHULA
MICKEY MANTLE